NO HANDS ALLOWED

A Robbie Reader

Freddy Adu
Young Soccer Super Star

Rebecca Thatcher Murcia

Mitchell Lane
PUBLISHERS

P.O. Box 196
Hockessin, Delaware 19707
Visit us on the web: www.mitchelllane.com
Comments? email us: mitchelllane@mitchelllane.com

Printing   1   2   3   4   5   6   7   8

A Robbie Reader
No Hands Allowed

Brandi Chastain	Brian McBride	DaMarcus Beasley
David Beckham	**Freddy Adu**	Josh Wolff
Landon Donovan		

Library of Congress Cataloging-in-Publication Data
Murcia, Rebecca Thatcher, 1962–
     Freddy Adu / by Rebecca Thatcher Murcia.
          p. cm. – (A Robbie reader. No hands allowed)
     Includes bibliographical references and index.
     ISBN 1-58415-385-7 (library bound)
     1. Adu, Freddy, 1989–Juvenile literature. 2. Soccer players–United States–
Biography–Juvenile literature. I. Title. II. Series.
GV942.7.A34M87 2005
796.334'092–dc22
                                                                              2004024612

ABOUT THE AUTHOR: Rebecca Thatcher Murcia grew up in Garrison, New York, and graduated from the University of Massachusetts at Amherst. She was a daily newspaper reporter–mostly in Texas–for 14 years. She is a soccer coach and player in Akron, Pennsylvania, where she lives with her husband and two sons. She is the author of other soccer biographies for Mitchell Lane Publishers, including *David Beckham* and *Landon Donovan.*

PHOTO CREDITS: Cover–Robert Laberge/Getty Images; pp. 1, 3, 4–Eric Miller/Getty Images; p. 6–Karim Jaafar/Getty Images; p. 8–Ville Myllynen/AFP/Getty Images; p. 10–Joe Murphy/WireImage; p. 12–Stan Honda/Getty Images; p. 15–Harry How/Getty Images; p. 16–Thos Robinson/Getty Images; p. 20–Jamie Squire/Getty Images; p. 22 (top)–Campbell's Soup Company via Getty Images; p. 22 (bottom)–Adam Pantozzi/WireImage; p. 25–Steve Grayson/WireImage; p. 26–Stephen Dunn/Getty Images; p. 27–Tony Quinn/MLS/WireImage.

TABLE OF CONTENTS

Chapter One
A Hat Trick at the Under-17 World Championship 5

Chapter Two
An African Childhood 9

Chapter Three
Heading Toward Stardom 13

Chapter Four
A Youth Superstar 17

Chapter Five
A Young Professional 21

Chronology 28
Glossary 29
Find Out More 30–31
Index 32

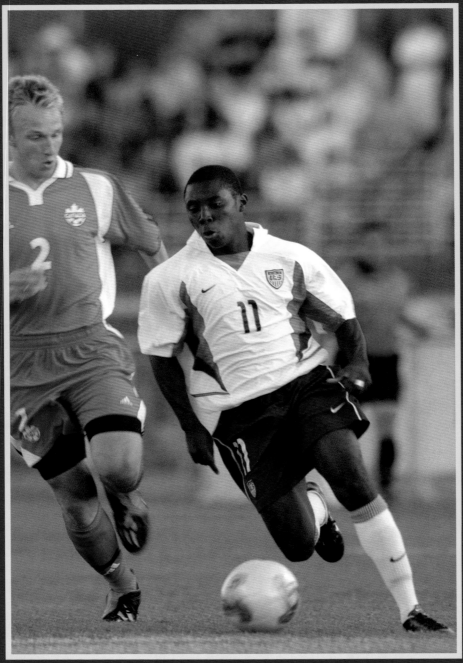

Freddy Adu is shown here playing for the United States Under-17 team against Canada. There has never been a young soccer player in America like Freddy Adu.

A Hat Trick at the Under-17 World Championship

Freddy Adu had to have been a little nervous. It was the first game of the Under-17 **World Cup** in Finland. Freddy's United States team had to face South Korea. South Korea had a good team. Two months earlier, they had beaten the Americans easily, 3-0.

Just 11 minutes into the game, one of the American players made a mistake and put the ball in his own net! The U.S. was losing 0-1. But Freddy, who was 14 years old, did not panic. He just kept playing hard. A few minutes later, an American player passed him the ball near the middle of the field. The South Korean goal was far away, but Freddy stayed calm. He ran

Freddy Adu was 14 when he scored three goals against South Korea at the Under-17 World Championship. Here he's trying to keep the ball away from a South Korean player.

with the ball. He dodged through the South Korean defenders. All he had to do was trick the goalkeeper and shoot. He did it! The Americans were tied 1-1 with South Korea.

The team still had a long game in front of them. They had to keep playing hard against very good players. They felt as though they could win. Other players scored. Near the end of the game, the U.S. was winning 4-1. Freddy scored again. Then a South Korean player knocked a U.S. player down. The referee gave the Americans a penalty kick. Freddy took it and scored. Freddy had a hat trick, or three goals in one game.

People watching the game were amazed. They had heard that Freddy was good, but now they had seen it with their own eyes. A 14-year-old had scored three goals to lead his team to a 6-1 victory in the first game of the Under-17 World Cup. It was hard to believe— but it is not the only part of Freddy Adu's story that is amazing.

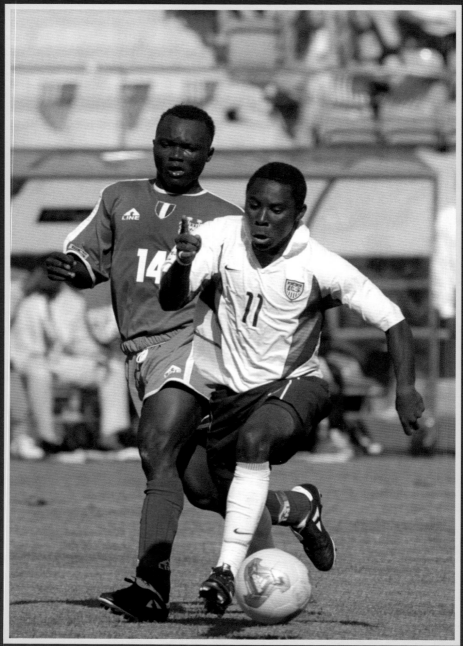

Here Freddy (front) is playing against Sierra Leone at the Under-17 World Cup. Freddy can do amazing things to get the soccer ball past defenders, but he also has a good sense of where his teammates are and can give them nice passes.

An African Childhood

Fredua Koranteng Adu was born on
June 2, 1989, in Tema, Ghana (GAH-nah).
Ghana is a small country in western Africa.
Many people have asked if Freddy could really
be as young as he says he is. *Sports Illustrated,*
a magazine, asked people in Ghana to look into
Freddy's age. The people could not find proof
that Freddy was born on June 2, 1989. But they
also could not find proof that he is older.

Freddy's parents are Emelia and Maxwell.
His younger brother's name is Fredua Akoto
Adu, but he is known as Fro. Fro would also
grow up to be a terrific soccer player.

Freddy did not have a soccer team in
Africa. He did not even have soccer shoes. He
played barefoot in the dirt in a neighborhood

Many young American soccer players have been inspired by Freddy's youth and talent. Here a boy holds up a homemade sign at D.C. United's game against the San Jose Earthquakes on April 3, 2004. D.C. United beat the Earthquakes 2-1.

park. He played with children and adults. He played and played and played. His mother said she lost count of all the soccer balls she bought for him. He would cry when she said that Freddy had to come inside for dinner at night.

Freddy was happy, but his mother wanted to make sure he went to good schools. When he was eight, his parents won an immigration visa lottery to move to the United States. The family moved into a small house in Potomac, Maryland. Their new life had begun.

11

At 14 years old, Freddy was the youngest person to play a professional team sport in more than a hundred years. Some experts said he was too young, but Freddy thought he was ready. This picture shows Freddy at the Madison Square Garden press conference in which it was announced that he signed a multi-year deal with U.S. Major League Soccer.

Heading Toward Stardom

When Freddy found out he was moving to the United States, he was excited. His cousins had told him good things about living there. Freddy was also worried. His friends said that kids in the United States did not like soccer. They said he would not get to play very much. At first, that was true. He tried to find children to play soccer with after school, but they usually wanted to play basketball.

At least there was one place where kids liked soccer: recess! He played soccer at recess and had fun. One day another child told his father, a soccer coach, about Freddy. Right away, Freddy got to play on a traveling soccer team called the Potomac Cougars. With Freddy on the field, dribbling, passing, and shooting, the Cougars were suddenly hard to stop.

Freddy was chosen to play on an Under-14 team in **tournaments** in Italy. In general, Italian soccer players are much better than American soccer players. But Freddy scored the most goals in the tournaments.

Scouts for rich Italian soccer teams watched Freddy play. They wanted to bring 11-year-old Freddy to Italy. They offered Freddy's mother many thousands of dollars. Her husband had left the family by this time. She was working two jobs to pay the bills. The family could have used the money, but Emelia said no. "I will not sell my son," she said.

Freddy also continued to do well in school. He won a **scholarship** to The Heights, a private school with a strong soccer team.

In 2001, Freddy led the Potomac Cougars to the Under-14 **national** championship. He scored four goals, the most of any player at his level. People were already talking about this amazing boy from Ghana. "He does not dribble the ball. He dances with it," wrote one soccer expert.

During Freddy Adu's first year as a professional player, older, stronger defenders did not want to let him score. Sometimes they did all they could do to stop him, such as in this picture: Troy Dayak of the San Jose Earthquakes is trying to hold Freddy back with his arm.

Freddy's mother, Amelia Adu (right), worked two jobs to support her family when Freddy was young. She taught Freddy to be very polite. Here they attend the AUDI Never Follow Gala in May 2004 at the Manhattan Center in New York City.

A Youth Superstar

Freddy was just beginning to be famous. The coach of the U.S. Under-17 team, John Ellinger, heard about Freddy and watched him play. "I couldn't believe my eyes," he said.

Ellinger asked Freddy and his mother if Freddy, then 12, could go to Bradenton, Florida, to train with the Under-17 national team. He would also study at a special high school there. Emelia did not want him to leave the house, but she decided to let him go.

Freddy fit in well with the teenage soccer stars at the school in Florida. He studied, but he also listened to music, watched movies, and played video games with the other boys. Julian Valentin, one of the other soccer players, said Freddy loved rap and hip-hop music. He liked to sing, but his voice was somewhat squeaky, according to Valentin.

Nike, a big sporting goods company, noticed Freddy's soccer skills. The company wanted him to wear its shoes and clothes. Nike asked Freddy's mother if the company could sponsor him. She said yes, and Nike gave Freddy's family about $1 million. His mother would not have to work so hard to support her family.

Before the Under-17 team could go to the world championship, they had to **qualify** by playing against other teams in North America. The team also practiced by playing against **professional** teams. In one game, an experienced professional defender almost fell down as Freddy dribbled by him.

The team won against Jamaica and Guatemala. They tied against El Salvador. Freddy had two goals and two assists, which are passes that lead to goals. The team went to Europe early to get ready for the Under-17

World Cup. Again, Freddy was a star as the team beat other youth teams in England.

After the team won its first game in the Under-17 World Cup, they faced bigger challenges. They won against Sierra Leone 2-1. In that game, Freddy scored a thrilling last-minute goal. He fooled the goalkeeper and then shot on an open net just before the game ended.

Brazil, which won the championship, beat the United States in the quarterfinals. The U.S. team went home without a trophy (TROH-fee), but Freddy had made a name for himself as one of the bright young stars in the world of soccer.

Freddy Adu played for the East at the Major League Soccer All-Star game on July 31, 2004. He controls the ball against Kerry Zavagnin of the West All-Star team. Freddy did not score a goal, but he played well.

A Young Professional

After a summer traveling in Europe and playing soccer, Freddy returned to school in Florida. He wanted to become a professional soccer player. He also wanted to finish high school. He studied a lot. In 2004, he did enough work to graduate at the young age of 14.

As Freddy studied, soccer fans everywhere wondered, What would Freddy do? In Europe he could become very rich. The American soccer teams did not have millions and millions of dollars like the teams in Europe. But Americans wanted him to stay in the United States. The soccer leaders made a plan. Freddy would earn $500,000 a year as a player for D.C. United, the professional soccer team in Washington, D.C. The pay was more than

In 2004, it was announced that Freddy Adu, a member of D.C. United of Major League Soccer, was signed to become a Campbell's spokesperson.

Freddy Adu has a reputation for being tireless and patient with fans and reporters. Here he poses with children before a game against the New York/New Jersey Metrostars.

anybody else in Major League Soccer. Freddy would be able to live at home with his family.

Other companies came looking for Freddy. He made a funny commercial with Pelé, the Brazilian who is known as the best player in the history of soccer. In that commercial, he juggled the ball with Pelé to see who would win the last bottle of soda. Then he made an even funnier commercial for Campbell's Soup.

Almost 25,000 people came to watch Freddy's first game as a professional. But they might have been a little disappointed. As D.C. United's older players took on the San Jose Earthquakes, Freddy watched from the bench. When he finally played toward the end of the game, he did not score a goal.

As the season wore on, Freddy's coach let him play more. Freddy kept getting better. He scored his first goal as a professional against the New York/New Jersey MetroStars at Giants Stadium on April 17, 2004. He played in the Major League Soccer All-Star game. A defender fell down when Freddy went by him, faking him out by stepping back and forth over the ball.

Toward the end of the season, D.C. United had an important game against the MetroStars. D.C. United won 1-0. Freddy scored the winning goal. He fired a rocket that hit a MetroStars defender and bounced into the goal. D.C. United ended the season by winning the Major League Soccer Championship in an exciting 3-2 victory over Kansas City Wizards.

Every time Freddy played, thousands and thousands of fans packed the stands. They often chanted, "Fre-dee! Fre-dee! Fre-dee!"

In December 2004, Freddy helped launch an after-school program that stresses the importance of exercise for kids. "I was lucky that I grew up in a neighborhood, both in Ghana and here in the States, where each day I could play soccer every chance I got," he said. "As a kid, being active and playing around is an important part of your childhood and I learned firsthand how much it can help you in keeping your body and mind healthy. I am happy to be part of NikeGO Afterschool so the kids in my hometown of Washington, D.C., and other cities will also benefit from being active and having fun."

At 15, Freddy was rich. He was famous. He was a fantastic soccer player. But his mother was still in charge. When she told him to each his vegetables, he did. After, all he would not be able to drive for another year.

Here Freddy dribbles the ball as Nick Garcia of the Kansas City Wizards chases after him. Freddy was thrilled about D.C. United's victory in the 2004 Major League Championships.

Sigi Schmid, the coach of the United States Under-20 men's team, chose Freddy as the youngest member of the team. The team will have to play very well to advance from the group stage. They face strong teams from Germany, Egypt, and Argentina.

Freddy Adu started the 2005 professional season looking a little stronger and heavier. He lifted weights two times a day during the off-season to build more muscle. Here he is in action during the CONCACAF Champions Cup on March 9, 2005.

1989 Born on June 2 in Tema, Ghana

1997 Moves to Potomac, Maryland

1999 Joins the Potomac Cougars

2000 Leads an Under-14 regional team to a tournament championship in Italy

2001 Goes to Bradenton, Florida, to train and study with the U.S. Under-17 national team; leads the Potomac Cougars to an Under-14 national championship

2003 Becomes a U.S. citizen; plays in the Under-17 World Cup in Finland and in the Under-20 World Championships in the United Arab Emirates; signs a $1 million contract with Nike

2004 Graduates from high school; plays professional soccer with D.C. United; helps launch an after-school program in Washington, D.C.

2005 Plays on the U.S. Under-20 national team that qualifies for the Under-20 World Cup, to be held in Holland

championship (CHAM-pee-un-ship)—an event at which a winner is declared the best of all the contenders.

national (NAH-shuh-nul)—having to do with an entire country.

professional (pro-FEH-shuh-nul)—a person who is paid to perform.

qualify (KWAH-lih-fye)—to be recognized as good enough to compete in a high-level game or tournament.

penalty kick (pen-el-TEE kik)—a direct kick on goal given to a team that is fouled inside a box in front of the opposing team's goal. The goalkeeper must wait on the goal line until the kick is taken.

scholarship (SKAH-ler-ship)—money awarded to pay for education.

tournament (TUR-nah-ment)—a competition with a series of games to eventually declare a winner, or champion.

World Cup (WERLD kup)—the international championship for outdoor soccer.

Articles

Drevitch, Gary, "Can't Miss Kid." *Sports Illustrated for Kids,* March 1, 2002, p. 54.

"Freddy Goes Professional: Adu Makes Historic Professional Soccer Debut with D.C. United." *The Connection Newspapers,* January 5, 2005.

Hernandez, Dylan. "Shadow of Fame: Freddy Adu's Brother." *Sports Illustrated for Kids,* June 1, 2004, p. T6.

Wright, Mark W. "Teen Dream." *Sports Illustrated for Kids,* July 1, 2004, p. 22.

Web Addresses

D.C. United
www.dcunited.com
Freddy Adu: The Soccer Phenomenon
www.freddyadu.net
Major League Soccer
www.mlsnet.com
U.S. Soccer Federation
www.ussoccer.com

Works Consulted

Borgenda, Volker. "Teen Star Adu Has U.S. in a Frenzy." *Sunday Times* (South Africa), July 18, 2004.

Canfora, Jason. "A 12-Year-Old's Amazing Feat: Soccer Prodigy Adu is Courted by Italy's Famed Inter Milan." *The Washington Post,* July 27, 2001.

DeSimone, Bonnie. "Adu on Cautious Track Toward Global Stardom." *Chicago Tribune,* May 31, 2004.

Rand, Michael. "A Class Above." *Star Tribune* (Minneapolis), July 11, 2003.

Wahl, Grant. "Who's Next? Freddy Adu: At 13, America's Soccer Prodigy Has the World at His Feet." *Sports Illustrated,* March 3, 2003.

_____. "Ready for Freddy?" *Sports Illustrated,* March 29, 2004.

Adu, Emelia   9, 11, 14, 16, 17, 18

Adu, Freddy
  birth   9
  childhood   9, 11
  moving to the United States   11, 13
  playing for the U.S. Under-17 team   4–8, 17, 18
  playing professional soccer   21–24

Adu, Fro   9

Adu, Maxwell   9

AUDI Never Follow Gala   16

Brazil   19

Campbell's Soup   22, 23

D.C. United   10, 21–24

El Salvador   18

Ellinger, John   17

Finland   5

Guatemala   18

Ghana   9–15

Heights, The   14

Italy   14

Jamaica   18

Kansas City Wizards   24, 25

MLS All-Star game   23

New York/New Jersey Metrostars   22, 23

Nike   18

NikeGO   24–25

Pelé   23

Potomac Cougars   13–14

Potomac, Maryland   11

San Jose Earthquakes   10, 15, 23

Schmid, Sigi   26

Sierra Leone   8, 19

South Korea   5, 7

Sports Illustrated   9

Under-14 team   14

Under-14 national championship   14

Under-17 World Cup   5–8, 18–19

Valentin, Julian   17, 18

Washington, D.C.   25